DIRT ROAD TO

SMOOTH PAVEMENT

Based on a True Story by Shannon Ben Dailey

Dirt Road to Smooth Pavement

www.LiveDailey.com

"Lack of direction, not the lack of time, is the problem.
We all have 24-hour days."

Zig Ziglar

CONTENTS

Acknowledgments

The hardest part in writing this book was to think of everyone who I wanted to thank for being a part of my life in some way. At first, I began to write acknowledgments about each person that has made an impact in my life and quickly discovered, pages and pages later, I wrote more in the acknowledgments than in the first two chapters of this book. So to keep it simple and sweet, I want to say thank you, thank you, thank you for every prayer, every hour of thought, for your time and conversation, for every meal, and just for being a part of my life and my family. Thank you to every person I have ever shaken hands with, to every person who challenged me intellectually and spiritually, that was patient with me and understood me.

Thanks to my family, friends, church members, acquaintances, employees, and peers. A special thanks to my outstanding wife, confidante, and friend, Domanicka; and to my three amazingly wonderful children: Taylor, Caleb, and Joshua. Thank you to such great parents, Ed and Sheila Dailey, and my brothers, Edward Jr. and Walter. I especially want to thank the One who knows me better than I know myself, my Lord and Savior Jesus Christ. If it wasn't for Him, I would not have parents, brothers, a loving wife, children, friends, and family with which to share my world.

Introduction

Leaving the Dirt Behind

When I look over my life and examine all the things that I have been through, I am amazed. How did this nerdy introvert—who despite making many poor choices and decisions in life, later turned from a mid-level hood rat into a business professional— consider my life to be a success story? I am choosing to tell my story because I believe those who read this book will realize that we all have done some things, or in my case a lot of stuff, that we are not proud of which have caused destruction to ourselves and to the lives of others. The good news is that the story continues on.

You have the ability to live your own happily ever after starting now, today! You have the power to change the very course or direction of your life at this very moment. Sure, it's going to require some work, sacrifice, discipline, and on and on. So knowing that change is going to require something from you, the question remains, "How badly do you want it?" How badly do you want to change from what once was or still is a destructive lifestyle to a life that is <u>constructive</u>? After all, we were created to live life happily ever after.

Dirt Road to Smooth Pavement is about the transitional success of a young man who began his journey in life as a drug dealer in high school, a college dropout, and a two-time felon who was transformed and became a successful trendsetter. My success is not only that I became a vice president of a regional retail chain business or later established, operated, and owned my own business for over six years, but also how my life literally changed mentally, physically, and spiritually.

Success for me and for you is not about just making money, but is about truly living the good life. In the midst of my poor choices and decisions, I did not know how to be a better person or to live the good life, so I was led most of the time by my instincts and past decisions—which was only a setup for future failures. On occasions when I did get support or direction, I was able to make better decisions and save time in the process.

Kathie Kuhn, one of my teachers, would say, "The more knowledge you have, the more choices you have." That statement is true knowledge and is powerful when used appropriately.

Help comes in a variety of ways. It may come through a person; the use of medication, if necessary; or, as for me, in a television show, an article, and books. My desire is that each person who reads this book will benefit or find help from the experience and knowledge I have gained thus far in my real-life journey. I trust that this book will provide knowledge, support, and direction on how to change for good and stay that way.

Finally, I want you to clearly understand that you are not alone when it comes to being rejected by society, acquaintances, family members, Human Resources Departments, or hiring managers because of your past mistakes. You are not alone when you feel less than important, isolated, or depressed in your life because of how you see yourself or how you think people perceive you. You are not alone in believing you will never get beyond a certain point in your life because of your past or the fear of making another mistake. I personally, as well as many others with troubled pasts, have been there and experienced it, too. Once you realize that you are not the only one, you can do what many others have done to overcome their past mistakes. You can set goals, make a plan to reach those goals, and most importantly, take action. Goals and plans are great ideas until you carry them out.

I believe this book will lend some relief that something better is waiting for each of us. Better is available right now if you want it. This book will illustrate how I overcame the stressful mental and physical challenges in my life. Discover what I learned as you find your own success and purpose in life.

1

Back in the Day

Here I sit inside the walls of a small, outdated office surrounded by file cabinets and beige partition walls on the west side of Cleveland. As I hear telephones ringing, fingers clicking on computer keyboards, and office personnel chattering in the background, I am sitting quietly by myself. I have about 15 minutes or so left to complete my basic math test to even qualify for the chance of being offered a temporary job as an entry level collector, which is a job I have never done before. According to my rep, this is the only position available, based upon my work history and background. I was really hoping for a management position with a corner office making $25 per hour with a company car. Instead, I had to settle for a low paying, entry level job with no benefits.

Sitting here on the brown metal folding chair, staring at my paper laying on the wood grain linoleum desktop, I begin to go into deep thought about my life thus far. I muscle up the courage to ask myself not just a question, but a series of questions regarding the past several years of my life. Why am I in this temporary placement agency in the first place? How could someone who is creative, intelligent, and with a great personality, come to such a place of despair? What do I need to do to prevent myself from ever coming back to this lowly position in life again?

The lowly place of despair I speak of is not being in the temporary agency looking for work, but is what I consider the lowest point in my life emotionally, mentally, physically, and spiritually. The poor choices I made had a direct impact on my present circumstances. In that moment, I had to decide whether I was going to return to the life to which I was accustomed, selling drugs and firearms; or do something "normal" like earn an honest paycheck, sit in rush hour traffic, and clock in and out for work, making not even close to the amount of money I was getting for selling drugs. Honestly, either choice made me nervous because there was no paid vacation, no medical benefits, or retirement pension fund running the streets. In most cases, you either retired in jail or in a grave, which I came close to experiencing on several occasions.

As for corporate America, I simply did not know what was required of me and what would happen if I failed to perform the task I agreed to. What if corporate America rejects me because I am not catching on, I am not educated enough to do the job, am not the right color, or gender? My very first job was a cook at a restaurant, then later I worked in a warehouse as an order picker.

Hustling was the only thing I felt that I was really good at doing, not to mention I did not have the skills or the business acumen to get a "real job." As these thoughts bombarded my mind, I quickly accepted that I cannot change my past, but I can definitely do something about my future. As I glanced at the multiple choice test once more, with time to spare, I began to recall what my life was like as a teenager.

I was raised in a very good home with my two brothers and both of my parents. Because my father was so devoted to keeping meals on the table and a roof over our heads, he often worked 10- to 12-hour shifts at an auto stamping plant on the south end of Cleveland. Since my Dad worked such long hours, my brothers and I only had a chance to be around him when he was home on the weekends. Most of that time was spent doing yard work—cutting grass, raking leaves, and shoveling snow—along with fixing things around the house.

On rare occasions, we would go fishing on his boat out on Lake Erie, which was a blast, or hunting in the woods, which I hated. My dad owned some land in Mesopotamia, Ohio, which we called Amish country. It was about an hour drive east of Cleveland off of Route 87. Amish country was like another world that we somehow teleported into, going from sidewalks, corner stores, and traffic to dirt roads, horses, and buggies. Out there, the skies seemed so blue; everything around me was so colorful, clean, and alive with nature.

I remember during the summer being in the back seat of my dad's Ford next to one of my brothers. I would have my arm hanging out of the window with the sun shining on my face as my dad cruised down Route 87 to get to his land. During hunting season, we would go out to his private property to hunt deer, rabbits, squirrels, or any other wildlife that moved. Getting to shoot the shotguns was awesome, but it was miserable standing out in the cold winter air. Waiting for something to shoot at was the least favorite part of the trip.

Once in a while, we would go on a family vacation to Ontario, Canada (which was the best time of my life as a kid). The whole family stayed together in a log cabin along the lake. My dad brought the boat along, so we could fish and dive into the lake from the boat. When we were not fishing, we hung out on the beach all day, eating all the sour cream and onion potato chips with RC Cola we wanted. Other times, we would visit my mom's family in West Virginia or my dad's family in Mississippi.

My mom was a Registered Nurse for the State of Ohio and maintained an active lifestyle. She belonged to a bowling league, loved to sew, and was very active in her church. Even though she was around more than my dad, my interaction with my mom consisted of her helping me with my school lessons and chores. Sometimes, on a school night, my little brother and I would go with her to watch her bowl at the local alley. She was really good at bowling. When we were not busy doing school work or watching my mom bowl, she would spend most of her time in her sewing room making all sorts of clothes, while fussing at the little 13-inch, black and white TV because some contestant guessed the wrong answer on a game show.

My little brother and I were big on fashion. I would flip through *GQ*, *Esquire*, *Essence*, and *Jet* magazines to observe and mimic what I saw. I used to love watching Morris Day and the group The Time on BET. They were not only good musicians, but also were cool and dressed to a "T." Morris Day would wear these shirts and suits that had various prints, like paisley, plaid, and houndstooth, with funky colors like burnt orange or lavender. We could not afford fashion like Morris Day, so my mom taught me how to sew my own paisley shirts and houndstooth pants. We would take trips to Jo-Ann Fabric where she would let me pick different materials with which to make my clothes.

When I wasn't sewing clothes with my mom, my younger brother and I, along with a couple of neighborhood kids, would spend our evenings playing kickball in the street, riding bikes in the neighborhood, playing Atari 2600, or playing musical instruments.

On Sundays, my mom, my little brother, and I went to church every single week, rain, sleet, or shine. My dad at that time felt he didn't need to go to church in order to go to heaven or to be a "good person," so he rarely, and I mean rarely, came to church. He would spend most of his days sitting on the far corner section of the couch next to his floor lamp, with his can of Schlitz malt liquor on the end table while reading the newspaper. He would sit back, with his reading glasses on and the paper open in between his hands just above his lap, and a cigarette hanging between his lips. That was my dad's Sunday ritual.

My older brother hardly ever, better yet never, attended church with us either. I would often find my older brother sleeping in on Sundays from being out all Saturday night. I often thought it was unfair he got to stay home from church, but after a while just simply accepted that was just the way it was. My older brother considered himself an outcast or the "black sheep" of the family. He was the independent, tough guy, yet was cool to be around. My older brother had a great sense of humor and was always cracking jokes or pranking someone. He often got into trouble with the local authorities for doing something devious or daring.

For as long as I could remember, I always looked up to him. In my eyes, he was a free spirit. He could do whatever he wanted, however he wanted, whenever he wanted. My older brother had a natural talent for mechanics and could repair or modify just about anything with an engine. He knew a lot about sports, politics, girls, and self-defense. He was very much into heavy metal music or anything with a distorted guitar solo. Growing up in a predominately African-American community in the '70s and '80s, it was unusual for an African-American male born and raised in the inner city of Cleveland to listen to hard rock music. If you were not listening to something "funky fresh" or "dope," you were not "cool or down."

My older brother, being the free-spirited person he was, listened to whatever he wanted; dressed how he wanted, with holes in his jeans and shirts with the sleeves ripped off; and would still manage to fit into any crowd. To me, that was cool.

As I got older, I became more independent, sort of like my older brother. During my junior high school years, I started going to a Pentecostal church on East 80th Street, which was one block east of Cleveland's worst projects, called Rainbow Terrace. I had several family members that lived in and around these projects. My dad would bring us with him for a visit. I never understood why my aunts and uncles chose to live there. These projects were notorious for drugs, prostitution, gangs, and violence. The police would not even patrol through this neighborhood after dark, and yet this was the area where I attended church with my best friend and his family, who lived a few houses down the street from my parents.

At the time, my parents were happy I was staying out of trouble by attending church, but they also didn't like it because this church was very different from the Baptist church my mother attended. They felt like it was an occult. We were in church all day Sunday then again on Wednesday night, which they really didn't like because it was a school night.

About a year after attending church, I got involved with the audio crew and formed a musical Christian band with my best friend. My little brother later joined the band, playing the keyboard. Our group traveled to many churches and to conventions to perform. It was great to play and sing original music that we wrote before audiences of all ages.

By the time I became a sophomore in high school, I dropped out of the band, stopped writing and playing music. I stopped going to church altogether. I stopped hanging out with my little brother and best friend. My little brother continued to faithfully go to this inner-city Pentecostal church and would ask me to come with him every Sunday, but I refused. I had no real reason why I stopped going to church. I led myself to believe that it was not cool to be a "Jesus freak." I started to believe I was missing out on life, partying, dating girls, and hanging with the guys because I was always at church. Also, being at church would not allow me to be more like my older brother, who I still looked up to.

When I was in the eleventh grade, I remember my older brother being in and out of jail for drug possession and domestic violence. At that time, I began to experiment with drugs recreationally, vowing that I would be very careful not to end up like my older brother, being in and out of jail, or being high on drugs all the time. Not only did I begin to use marijuana, but also I began to sell it. It didn't stop there. I started to hang around gang members from different gangs around the city. Because my high school was downtown, I met people from all over Cleveland and had no allegiance to any one place or group. Besides, I never joined a gang because I personally didn't see the logic or benefit of joining, but that still didn't stop me from selling drugs and weapons to them.

Church was in my rearview mirror, fading fast into the landscape. From time to time, I would talk to my little brother to see how he was doing, and give him money, clothes, or anything else he wanted. Occasionally, he would update me on what was happening with certain people in the church and where the band was playing. A lot of times after talking to my brother, I felt convicted for trading God for the streets. I often felt like I made a huge mistake, but I couldn't stop myself. On top of that, I knew he had no idea how far gone I was into hustling the streets. With the repeated use of drugs, alcohol, partying, and girls, I became emotionally dead and no longer recognized how far I had slid into a world of crime and destruction.

Shortly after graduating from high school, I attended college in Atlanta for about one semester. I went to this particular college because it was a very popular school and seemed to be the right decision, since they were the only college to accept me on an academic probation. College seemed to be the right decision at the time, but once I got there, I realized I was way out of my league. That school was not for me. Even though the parties were wild and crazy, I began to feel guilty for wasting my parents' money. However, I rarely studied, let alone went to class. I was having a good time partying. Not only that, it was hard to make money selling drugs when just about everyone I met there already had their own drug connection.

So I decided to go back home and transfer to a community college in Cleveland. My time there was not very long before I dropped out of college altogether. I really did not want to go to college. I only went because my parents were pressuring me to do so, and I didn't want to disappoint them. Needless to say, my parents were very disappointed when I dropped out after only three combined semesters of college.

Originally after high school, I was planning to go into the Air Force. I remember taking the ASVAB test in the library at my high school and passing it. I was so excited because my dad was also in the Air Force, and I wanted to follow in his footsteps. He used to talk about how he traveled the world and how great it was to explore new things, places, and people. As exciting as I thought my life was as a petty dealer, I knew I took a wrong turn; and if there was a way to get on track, joining the Air Force would be it. The recruiting officer came to my parents' home. They talked and talked as I just sat and listened on the staircase opening next to the living room where my parents and the recruiter were.

My dad and the recruiter talked military jargon while my mom interjected periodically. Days later, after the recruiter came to my parents' house, my dad called for me. I ran up the stairs from the TV room in the basement to see what he wanted. My dad stood in the kitchen in front of the sink, looking out of the window toward the backyard and said, "Son, I know you want to do something with your life, but I don't think it's a good idea for you to go into the service right now because there are major wars brewing in the Middle East." The wars he was talking about were the Persian Gulf War and the Afghan Civil War. He said that he was concerned about the chemical warfare that was already happening. I was really shocked by what my dad was saying because I thought he would at least be happy that I wanted to do something with my life in service to my country. I was speechless and didn't know how to respond.

College was what they wanted for me. They were hoping I would be the first in our family to earn a degree, since my older brother blew that chance by being in trouble with the law so much. I later found out the dream for one of us to earn a degree was because no one else in my family has ever earned a degree.

After I dropped out of college, I lived with my parents for a while. I led my family to believe that I was working hard, so that one day very soon I would be able to be on my own. I wanted to make them proud of me, and I desperately wanted to make up for being a disappointment to them when I dropped out of college. I thought the only way they would be proud of me again was to prove to them that I could make my own money, regardless of how I made it. First, I worked at a restaurant for a short period of time. Then I quit the restaurant and began working at a factory, all while running the streets at night. I was living a secret life. My family had no idea that I had been selling drugs and performing other criminal activities since high school. In reality, the "odd jobs" were a front. They were only a means for me to continue selling drugs in a more discreet manner; and so I did, and did it well.

2

A Job Within a Job

At this point in my life, I could not have cared less about earning an honest living. In fact, I was believing my own lies that I told my parents in order to mask the emotional disappointment of my parents not being happy with their dropout son. This was even though I was doing well at work and got promoted from labor worker to team leader, then floor supervisor. My real focus was on my drug deals and that income, which far exceeded my weekly paychecks I received from my job.

Work was like the opening of Pandora's box. What I mean by that is comparing my job to selling drugs on the streets and hanging out at corner stores waiting for buyers, which was extremely risky. It was risky because you didn't know if the buyers were undercover agents, petty dealers posing as addicts, or snitches working for the local task force.

In the workplace, the clientele was completely different. I couldn't believe how easy it was to sell to so many under one roof. I was amazed by the number of people doing drugs in corporate America. There were parents; people of power; and people of responsibility, like office executives and plant and shift managers; plus a couple of thousand employees. I thought wanna be drug dealers, recreational users, and addicts were my only target market, which were those to whom I normally sold. Instead, in corporate America I found my niche, and it was all mine. I found my hustler's paradise, which was ordinary people who worked eight or more hour shifts per day, five to six days per week that came directly to me to get high on my products.

I looked forward to reporting to work every day, especially on payday. Every week, employees would cash their checks at the local deli shop where there was a check cashing window in the back of the store. My coworkers would line up to pay a fee to a clerk to cash their checks. Employees would get their liquor and groceries for the weekend and stock up on my drugs. I even offered a line of credit to many of my frequent users. It got to a point that I knew who wanted what and how much they wanted without them asking me.

I was a junior in high school when I first began selling joints and dime bags to students and a couple of teachers. As I entered the working class community, I went from joints and dime bags to pounds of marijuana each week. I mainly sold pounds of marijuana, a decent amount of crack to my coworkers, and cocaine to several executives in the front office. I also sold weapons. My clientele was growing at a fast pace because of the quality of what I sold and the convenience. I was making more money than ever compared to street sales, not including distribution sales to other drug dealers. At the rate I was going, I thought that selling dope was something I could do for the rest of my life.

I convinced myself, my parents, and others outside of the secret society of drugs I had a high paying job. As strange as it may seem, this was my way of making amends for dropping out of college and wasting my parents' money. And that was the story I told myself. I was hoping that my supposedly high paying job would somehow overshadow my dropping out of college and would put it completely out of my parents' minds.

I quickly stepped up to being the professional to this working class clientele by being discreet and staying clean. Beyond not doing drugs, I changed the way I handled myself. I walked tall, with my shoulders squared, and had a firm handshake. I changed how I talked. I would look the person directly in the eyes when talking, use no slang, nor use the "N" word. I also changed how I dressed. I wore my shirts tucked in, pants around my waist, was clean cut and well groomed. I didn't sport the latest J's, or big rope chains, at work. I kept my appearance simple. Finally, I changed the type of car I drove. I had a nice Cadillac Eldorado that I drove when I was just hanging out (which was rare); and I had a hooptie, which was an old Chevy Cavalier hatchback that had no air conditioning, no power door locks or windows, that I drove every day to work and to make my rounds on the streets. No one taught me or told me what to do; it was pure instinct from being a people watcher. I adapted quickly.

In high school, a lot students did not know that I was a dealer. I was nerdy, introverted, and soft spoken. I kept to myself and was big into fashion. The guy that got me started into selling drugs was in my social studies class. He was in a gang and was built like a running back. He always wore white K-Swiss, Levi's jeans, and a white t-shirt. He liked that I was not like the others who were trying to sell drugs for him. The other kids were roughnecks, or at least they were trying to be. I often saw them in the principal's office when I would pass by. Me, I was still nerdy, laid back, and wearing preppy clothes.

In the workplace, I was very discreet and kept a low profile but was firm and direct, unlike high school days. I never dressed like a thug, nor did I act like one. Getting started in corporate America was like reading a nutritional label on a bag of potato chips. I had to read the label of drug and substance abuse in the faces and body language of my coworkers in order to know to whom to offer or suggest drugs. I could easily tell if someone was using drugs from the combination of stress lines around their eyes, the dark crusty color of their lips, or even the brown marks on their fingertips. Nervous and anxious behavior were also indicators as to who was onboard for drug activity. Even though I was tactful in my solicitation, I had to be very careful not to ask the wrong person or to misinterpret the way a person looked, so that I would not expose my operation. It was a secret society in the workplace of users who were very sensitive about their extracurricular activities. Once I got in good with a couple of users, they turned me on to many others in the workplace. Normally, these users would ride the streets looking for drugs that I provided.

After a while, I no longer had to read people for drug and substance abuse. I had plenty of referrals contacting me regularly for drugs. With a company that had over 2,000 employees, including the front office, management, and three shifts, I felt I would not be able to keep up with the supply and demand at work. Therefore, I recruited a few guys and a gal that would think and act like me in order to keep the distribution going quietly during the hours of operation. Because of the increasing amount of drug sales activity, I had to be more alert than ever not to let my guard down. I had to always be watching my recruits in case of a double cross, or new employees that could rat me out or become my competition.

At some point, not only could I tell who used drugs, but also I could tell who was lying about their boring weekend, who was about to get fired, or those desperately looking for an escape. I paid special attention to the loud and obnoxious people. Initially, they were my target if they had money to spend on alcohol in order to become the life of the party at a happy hour; I knew that they could afford my drugs. Sometimes I was hesitant to sell to those who were always in the limelight because they were people I regarded as high risk. This type of person typically had more than just my eyes watching them. Mid and upper level management would monitor them closely as well. I was very cautious about doing business with them.

Overall, I was still stunned at the number of people who got high and how frequently they would purchase even more narcotics from me, especially when it came to the white collar executive who was a family man. He had awards and trophies for a job well done. He had pictures of his wife and kids hung on the wall of his office. He had a nice car, lived in the suburbs, had a family, and a good job. For the life of me, I could not understand why he was doing drugs. Needless to say, before his business trips, he always got a little extra before leaving.

Then there was the struggling single mom who would often get a ride to work or even sometimes catch the bus because her car was always in the shop or her man had it when, in reality, it had been repossessed. When I would see her in the cafeteria, she was usually eating Ramen noodles or an item she would pack for her kid's lunch. When payday came, she would be one of the first in line to spend her light bill money on getting high.

And then there was the guy who got paid on Friday and was broke by Saturday night. As broke as he was, he managed to find money to purchase more drugs from me during the week.

Employees like those I mentioned kept coming back two and three times a week for more drugs. Being exposed to people like the family man, struggling mom, and the guy who was always broke was a challenge for me at first because, in their cases, they were working to support their families. I felt the last thing they should do was get involved with someone like me. Therefore, I quickly learned to leave my emotions out of the game altogether. It was none of my business what they would do with their money or what they would do with their lives. There is no such thing as a successful emotional dealer. People would nickel and dime your emotions if they recognized it. They would tell you anything or were willing to do anything to get their high. They would plead their cases as to why they should get something on credit. Relatives always expected to get something free. People I grew up with thought because they knew me or knew of me that I should just automatically hook them up.

It did not matter to me if they were friend or foe; I treated everyone the same. I trusted no one. I treated everyone as if they were liars and could not be trusted. And I was the best liar of them all. After all, I was able to look my parents, family, and people who knew me growing up straight in the face and tell them what they wanted to hear without blinking or looking away from them. Since I was the best liar of them all, I could detect a liar in the act. I was on my way to becoming a skilled illegal entrepreneur.

3

Didn't See It Coming

It had been almost four years since I first began selling drugs in high school. During that time, I saw many drug dealers and street corner hustlers come and go and not even last a year in the streets. As a result, I felt untouchable. *I am in control*, I thought. There were a lot of envious people out there waiting for my fall, like a defending boxing champ that was surprised by an upper cut that put him on the canvas. In the streets, two kings cannot rule the same block; one will eventually overthrow the other and will use any resources to do so.

Often, competing drug dealers would use a snitch, who was typically a drug addict. Drug dealers, including myself, would use these addicts to communicate to Cleveland's finest details about local dealers, schedules, activities, and operations. If you can use a snitch or turn an informant against your competition, you can get the law to do the heavy lifting for you. However on the flip side, police officers and task forces have been known to offer a snitch or informant a "get out of jail free" card just for staging a setup to capture dealers. Most snitches would go for these deals, but tend to play both sides because they get the best of both worlds: police protection while they stay on their crack diets from drug dealers.

Over the course of time, I outlasted many of my competitors with the help of a snitch or informant. Most of my competition was either in jail, had been killed, or had become addicts themselves. Most dealers would get high just to camouflage the fear of being caught or murdered and the stress of everyday survival on the streets and always being on the run. I had earned my respect in the streets and in the workplace simply by being smart and discreet. In the business world, one of the ways you can judge the success of a company is by how long they have been in business. There was a saying I heard, which is 90% of startup businesses will fail within the first five years of doing business. Well, in my opinion, in the streets, instead of five years, over 90% of those selling drugs would either be dead or in jail within the first two years. Because of this statistic, I handled myself differently. I limited the amount of alcohol and personal interaction, so I could stay focused and on top of my game, until this particular summer night.

It was Wednesday evening after work, and I was on my way home. I stopped at a night club and a couple of bars to make sure my local dealers were doing well and the club owners and managers were being taken care of. This was my usual custom every other night. As I was passing through a suburb on the east side of Cleveland, I was waved down by a local junkie who knew my older brother. They were like best friends since childhood. Because he and my brother were close, in spite of him being a local junkie, I always treated him like a neighborhood friend. The local junkie was crossing into the intersection that I was approaching, wearing a dirty green trench coat, and waving his hands in the air to flag me down.

My golden rule was to never, ever stop for anyone on the block, especially for a junkie at an intersection. My first instinct was to keep driving, which is what I did; but for some odd reason, as I proceeded to drive past him, I stopped the car. I'd known this dude most of my life, and he was close friends with my older brother. He quickly walked up to my car. I rolled down the passenger window halfway, and I turned the volume down low on my radio, so I could hear what he wanted or had to say to me. He started rambling and not making sense, as if he was nervous about something or just high. Then he finally said he was cold and needed a ride, but he didn't say where he was going on this calm and chilly summer evening. I told him he needed to walk faster if he needed to stay warm because he was not getting into my car. I let my foot off of the brake pedal as the car slowly started to coast off. And as I began to roll up the window, but before I could reach for the knob to turn my music back up, the junkie—with one hand on the windshield and the other on the passenger window—stuttered over his words, and said he had something to tell me about my older brother.

I immediately stopped, thinking something must have happened to my older brother because this junkie knew not to waste my time, and it had been weeks since

I had talked to my older brother. I reached over the passenger seat to pull on the door handle of the passenger door to let him into the vehicle. I watched the junkie reach for the passenger door handle as I leaned back into my driver's seat with anticipation, hoping to hear that my older brother had not been shot or was in a hospital somewhere.

Just as soon as he pulled on the handle to open the passenger side door, I was instantly surrounded by agents that had raided a couple of drug houses a block away in this middle class community. I was startled because one moment it was me and this junkie, and in the next moment, it was like ninjas dropped down out of trees and off of the houses as they quietly and quickly surrounded my car. I can still remember the touch of cold steel from a 12 gauge shotgun barrel poking me on the side of my head through the driver's side window, which was already rolled down. The agent behind that gun had just pumped a live round into the barrel. Using profane language, he dared me to move any part of my anatomy while his partner read me my rights, all the while yelling at the top of his lungs with his gun jabbing me on the side of my head.

One thought that ran through my mind was that dude on the other end of the gun had to be on drugs because he wouldn't shut up. Then the next thing I thought is that I should have been scared or even intimidated, but instead I was getting angry, frustrated, and a bit mouthy, daring the officers to do what they must while I was gripping the steering wheel with both hands. I was not caught in the act of a criminal transaction or dealing. So why were they reading me my rights? Unless talking to a junkie was illegal, what proof did they have on me for doing something criminal?

The agents were literally trying to force me out of my car through the driver's side window, only to realize I could not fit through the window because of my seat belt, not to mention the car was in drive with my foot on the brake. So then they shoved me back into the car while the officer was still yelling, with his 12 gauge still pointed at me. They opened the driver's side door, put the car in park, and unbuckled my seat belt. Coming out of my vehicle hands first, I stood up by the car with one agent on each side of me. They took me to the curb and laid me face down on the tree lawn and frisked me. They put handcuffs on my wrists behind my back, while other agents continued to search the vehicle. They pulled apart the panels of my car doors, searched through every compartment in the trunk, and checked under the frame of my car while removing the rear car seats from the vehicle. All of this took place right at this neighborhood intersection while people slowly cruised by the scene to see what was going on.

Suddenly, after they trashed my car, an officer called out to the other agents to come to the passenger side of my car where he found what appeared to be about an ounce of marijuana, rolled up in a plastic sandwich bag, stashed somewhere on the passenger side. I knew it did not belong to me and, furthermore, they ripped my car apart only to find this bag on the floor of the passenger side? There was only one way that I transported drugs, and it was not accessible from inside the car. Yes, I had drugs in the car, but they did not find what actually belonged to me during their search. It was at that very moment I knew this was staged. In unbelief, I thought, *Was it the junkie who set me up? The guy who was best friends with my older brother? The same guy that knew me most of my life? Who mysteriously vanished into thin air during the raid?* He was nowhere to be found at the scene, and there was no way to prove the marijuana did not belong to me.

With handcuffs already around my wrists, one of the agents then cuffed my ankles, grabbed me up off the lawn, and proceeded to drag me around the corner to a drug house that they raided prior to my arrest. As we approached the house, it dawned on me (which made me even more irate) that the house they raided was right around the corner from where I had stopped, and I had not even noticed this prior to the junkie running up to my car. Not only that, but the junkie who set me up lived across the street from the house they had raided. I only knew this because when I was first starting up my illegal drug business, this junkie's house used to be a drop-off for drugs to the local dealers for me.

Inside the house they raided there were about 15 people or so handcuffed and sitting on the floor; some were local drug dealers, casual users, and junkies the agents caught. What appeared to be an armored bus pulled up and stopped in front of the raided house with several other police cars. They had us all chained two by two with one another and proceeded to move us from the house they raided onto the bus in the front yard. Just before I stepped aboard the bus, I looked back. Through the backyard of the house that they raided, I saw my car still in pieces at the intersection with a couple of police officers standing near the scene. I could not believe that this had happened to me. I looked away to step onto the bus heading for the Fourth District Precinct to be processed.

It was quiet and seemed to be a very long ride on that bus to get to the Fourth District building. Once we got to the Fourth District, the bus went underground. Suddenly, quiet sounded more like panic, judging by the expressions of those on the bus cuffed with me. Once they got us off the bus and inside to the main holding area, it was total chaos. People were talking loud, some people were crying, others were telling their stories as to how they got caught and how long they had been running from the police. For some, it was a reunion. People were laughing and cracking jokes with each other. Guys were yelling over who had the best gang and who they were going to shoot when they got out. Needless to say, I did not sleep one bit from all the commotion.

A couple of days later, I was transferred to the tenth floor of the Justice Center Jail in downtown Cleveland. This floor was known to incarcerate hardcore criminals for federal crimes or murders. I stayed on this floor for a day. I thought they put me on this floor to scare me or something. The crime I was charged with did not warrant a visit to the tenth floor. Unlike the Fourth District, the tenth floor was creepy, with the dungeon look of gray walls and worn paint on the cell bars. You knew something or someone was there watching you, but you could not see it or them.

It was in that very tight, one-cot jail cell that I kept replaying in my head the whole scene of me getting set up. I kept asking myself how I could have let my guard down. I could not believe this junkie did this to me. He had known me since I was a kid riding on a big wheel. He and my older brother were boys; at least I thought they were.

Almost 48 hours after the night I was set up, I was released from the county jail on bail. I had not reported to work since Wednesday. When I finally got to work the day after I made bail, I was immediately pulled into the manager's office. I just knew that I was already fired. I could not come up with a good enough excuse as to why I had missed the past couple of days of work. Instead, much to my surprise, I was written up for a no call or show for not being at work, with a final written warning to not call off or be late for the next 60 days. I was grinning from ear to ear because I knew I should have been fired. Since I had perfect attendance and was a hard worker prior to this incident, I was given another chance to continue to work.

I was relieved because I did a lot to build up my clientele for drug sales at this company, and I did not want to lose the steady income I had created. Besides, no one knew what happened to me, not even the guys I recruited to help me sell in the workplace; and I wanted to keep it that way until I figured out what to do next. The only people that missed me were the employees I worked with.

I finally made it to the impound lot on the west side of Cleveland to get my car back. After I left the impound lot, I pulled over to a nearby park area, anxious to check to see if my stash was still safely tucked away. And it was all there and accounted for. As I put the seats and paneling back in place from the police ripping it out, I just smiled the whole time. I knew that if the agents had only found this stash—which was much more than what they caught me with—I would have definitely been sent to prison and not just been given a couple of nights in the county jail.

4

Criminal Redemption

I needed to get myself together. I had not been in court to be tried as a convicted felon since I made my plea at the arraignment hearing about a month before. I did not know what to expect. My attorney gave me some general scenario of what might possibly happen. Whatever happened, I was surely hoping I did not get locked up for this. I heard the bailiff calling my name faintly, and again a little louder and clearer, and once more loud and clear, MR. SHANNON DAILEY! My attorney turned his head to see why I had not stood up after I had been summoned by court personnel, and there was a gallery of people waiting for me to rise up out of my seat.

As I snapped out of the daze that I was in, I slowly stood up before the judge, and wiped my face as the judge began speaking to me. I could see his lips moving, but I could not hear anything that he was saying. I could not hear him because I was still rehearsing what happened that night. Then instantly with clarity, I heard the judge say to me that my lawyer argued my case very well. In my mind, he had better have argued my case well after I spent thousands of dollars for him to keep me from being sentenced to prison.

Suddenly there was a still, eerie silence that came over the courtroom that lasted for what felt like several minutes after the judge finished his statement. It felt like something really bad was about to happen. Then the judge said with a very firm voice, "I sentence you to 18 months in a correctional facility." My heart started beating fast to faster and loud, and I felt a rush of heat through my body as I tried to look cool, as if what he said didn't faze me as he stared sharply into my eyes. I was trying to remain cool, but I felt like I could not catch my breath. All I could think about was how in 18 months the criminal empire that I had established would be gone. My reputation would be tainted forever in the streets. You would think at this point that I would have been remorseful, but I wasn't; or I would have seen the light after getting caught, but I did not. And what about my parents? They would soon discover the truth about my lie. It would break their hearts to know that not only had their first child been in trouble with the law but also their middle boy had.

After a brief pause, the judge continued on to say, "Due to this being the very first crime you have ever been convicted of, the court will forgo your 18-month sentence to jail. Rather, you will be referred to one year of probation.

I turned and looked at my attorney, who had a smirk on his face and in his mind was saying, *Will that be cash or charge?* because this particular attorney did not care about me. It was all about the money. As he looked at me, his smirk became a smile on his face, and then he said, "You are a free man, but not really." That statement stuck with me until this day. He shook my hand and mentioned he had another appearance to make, and immediately left to go and defend another criminal in the same building. As he shook my hand, he had this look of expectation or maybe confidence. He looked as though he knew I was going to return to the streets again only to get caught, just so he could be my attorney and collect several thousand dollars in fees.

Shortly after the hearing, I had to report to the Parole Office at the Justice Center in downtown Cleveland. I heard a lot of interesting stories about this place and was not looking forward to being there; but then again, it beat an 18-month sentence. Each month, I would go downtown to visit my parole officer in his very small office with a tiny window near the ceiling. He never looked me in the eyes nor asked me how I was doing. There was never any casual conversation between us. His only concern, as he rattled through his desk drawer, was to look for his box of latex rubber gloves he used to handle urine samples. Of course, he was testing whether or not there were drugs in my system. I casually drank and smoked a little, but during my probationary period, I did not smoke, drink, nor was in a room or place where others did so. I managed to stay clean from that point forward, and because this was my first offense, I definitely didn't want to do anything to overturn the judge's decision not to put me in jail.

In 12 months of routine visits, the probation officer never once asked me if I had a job, was staying out of trouble, or was under the influence of any alcohol or substance. For all he knew, I could have been right back to my criminal ways, selling drugs and running the streets, which I was. However, month after month, it was the same ritual. I would drive down to the Justice Center to sign a piece of paper and wait in line for about a half an hour or more to pee in a cup. After a while I stopped complaining because I could have been in the state prison instead of being at the Parole Office. Needless to say, ironically, there was always someone present in the lineup discreetly offering to sell his urine just in case you knew your sample would not pass the drug screening. I always thought that person was an undercover cop; besides, did people really purchase urine?

After I left the Parole Office, I would go straight to work, and it was business as usual. Now that I was back in business, I had a new agenda—to seek and destroy. I had to find and murder this junkie for setting me up. I spent a lot of time plotting and planning how I was going to kill him and dispose of him and any evidence. I wanted him to pay. I wanted him to feel my pain and embarrassment with a .380 caliber slug lodged in his chest from my chrome polished, pearl handle handgun. I wanted him to experience what it was like to have a hostile and angry person with a gun aimed at his head, only I was not going to just threaten him like the agent threatened me. This junkie was going to die for the simple fact that he humiliated me, and this was my way of revenge. From that point on of him setting me up, I lost brownie points in the streets. Other dealers were starting to think that I was weak and could be pushed around because I allowed that junkie to get into my head. So murdering the junkie would be my criminal redemption. Once I was done with the junkie, the local dealers were next on my hit list.

As for the junkie, no one would miss him when he was gone. He had no friends, family, nor next of kin who would care. He was a junkie, so who cared? I convinced myself that killing him would at least make me feel better and redeem some of the street credit or respect I lost. I had a well thought out plan on how I was going to kill him, where I would hide his body, and dispose of the weapon and tools used. I would reenact my plan in my head daily. I was obsessed. Months of searching became almost a year of looking for this junkie. My hatred for him grew every day, and the fact that I could not find him infuriated me. The desire to murder him was more intense the longer it took to find him. I was becoming obsessed. I searched every crack house and every known place where he or a junkie would be. After nearly a year of searching, I could not find him. I just assumed he overdosed or someone else took him out before I could get to him. After a while I decided to move on from tracking this junkie down.

I could not let go of the obsession to hurt someone, as if the drugs I was selling were not enough. In some twisted way, I wanted to physically hurt people as if I was making others pay for what this junkie did to me. I figured the local dealers got this junkie and the police involved in my life, and now it was time for some payback. My crew and I began to randomly break into local drug dealers' homes and apartments, robbing and beating these dealers senseless. We took everything from cars, money, and jewelry, and sometimes even their clothes. I recall times we dragged a half-naked dealer into the middle of the street just to humiliate him. This was better than selling drugs.

My obsession turned into jealousy, which turned into the lust for power and eventually led me to fear. Even though hardly anyone knew it was me and my crew doing all these random robbings and beatings, I feared that somehow or some way these local dealers would catch on or find out it was me, and in turn would go after me, my brothers, or even worse, my parents. After all, I was in a world where there were no rules. At any point in time, one of my crew members could have sold me out to the highest bidder of any of these local dealers we hit.

I kept envisioning myself being shot and killed repeatedly, night after night, by the dealers I had robbed and beaten. I told no one about these dreams. At times, I would purposely not go to sleep to avoid dreaming. I had insomnia, or when I did sleep, the dreams I repeatedly had made me feel paranoid. Rumors were floating around the hood about dealers getting robbed and beaten, which made me even more paranoid, due to attention on our criminal extracurricular activities. I lessened my involvement in robbing dealers, even though members of my crew continued. I started distancing myself from my crew, and over time, we went our separate ways.

I was being tormented by demons. The dreams kept coming, but instead of dreaming about getting killed, I was also dreaming about the crimes I had committed, along with the faces of people I had hurt over the years. I was getting sloppy at doing my warehouse job, and on occasion showed up late for work. The guys that were selling for me at the warehouse stepped up and ran things at work and just paid me my premium each day.

Any light that was ever shining in me was completely gone at this point. I was in total darkness to the point I was no longer me. My body and mind were controlled by darkness. I felt like Jesus was knocking on the door of my heart, but I did not want to answer. Instead, I was peeking through the window of my heart, like a peephole in a door, to see who it was. I no longer knew who I was or what I stood for. I could see the image of being a legitimate working class man saying, "One day, that will be me, but not today."

5

Webs We Weave

There was a cabaret being hosted by a local radio station, one of those B.Y.O.B. (bring your own bottle) parties which was packed wall to wall with people, old school hip hop, food, and tons of liquor. It had been a while since I been out to a club or had a life. That night I met a woman who was several years older than me. She came with a friend or two, and I could tell they dragged her out to this party that night. I invited her out on the dance floor, and then afterwards we sat down and had a couple of glasses of wine; and she began to tell me why she would have rather been at home listening to Sade. She mentioned she had just gotten over a terrible divorce and that she had a brother who was living with her for a short while to help her with the mortgage payments and utilities. She was worried that she was going to lose her home because of financial issues.

I thought to myself, *Either I am drunk, or she is, or both.* She shared way too much information with me for this not to be an official date. We talked a lot about her that night. She did not ask much about me. I was completely fine with her not asking any questions because I was not ready to lie to her or share with her the truth about what I had done over the past several years of my life, let alone the past two hours before I got to the cabaret. After the party, we exchanged numbers. As we parted, I felt strange because I began to feel emotions that I had not felt in a very long time. I had been with women but not a lady. That night around her made me actually feel human, like I could care for her or have a serious relationship with her. It felt strange because I was accustomed to being alone with the shallow relationships

I was a part of. For the first time in a long time, it felt good to be wanted as a normal person and not for the things I had.

I needed a change in my life; I needed to slow down and get a grip on myself. I thought if I would just get married, that would slow things down for me. It would get me out of the streets and make me stop selling. As extreme and desperate as I was to change my wicked ways, which I didn't realize they were at the time, I felt marriage would be my golden ticket.

A few weeks had passed since we met at the cabaret. We would talk on the phone and meet at a club, but she absolutely did not want me to come to her house or to meet her brother that was living with her. As the weeks passed and she still did not want me to come to her house, I began to wonder if this was a sign that I should not be involved with her. I must have been out of my mind to think that a serious relationship, let alone marriage, would solve any of my problems or make these demons in my life go away.

Finally, after weeks of seeing her, it all made sense why she did not want me to come to her house. I discovered she had two little children and was going through a custody battle with her ex-husband, who she divorced some time before. She did not want to jeopardize any chance of getting custody of her children. Also, I think she was afraid to tell me about her children because she thought that by me knowing she had kids, that would have scared me away when we first met. I think she may have been right on that account. She said she did not want her children to see another man in her house until we were more serious about each other. I was fine with that because I was not prepared for a "ready-made family." I just wanted to slow down, not be a daddy.

As easy as it would have been to walk away from her, there was something about her that kept me coming back. I concluded that for the first time in a long while the conversations we had allowed me to tap into my emotions, and I enjoyed it. Deep down, I missed that side of me. Because I was in so much darkness, even the dimmest artificial light was bright enough to feel again. We dated for several months and then it happened; we got married. I loved her for who she was, but I knew I was not in love with her. I was never in love before, so I thought maybe it would just take time for me to be struck by that type of emotion. Deep down, I knew I married her only to fix something that was broken in me, not realizing I married her for all the wrong reasons, for selfish reasons.

During the marriage, I hardly saw her or her children. As time progressed, we argued more than we would casually talk. We argued over things that later we would forget what we were arguing about in the first place. The problem in our marriage was that we never knew each other or even tried to truly get to know each other like married couples should. Not only did we not know each other, but also we were both dealing with our own personal demons. She thought I was a union warehouse worker that worked a lot of hours and carried a concealed weapon for protection. She also knew my parents did not approve of us getting married at all, but we tried to make something work between us anyway. Here I was again living a secret life that my family, and now my wife, knew nothing about. Our relationship was built on a fabricated life, a complete lie. There was no trust or honesty among us.

I knew our marriage had come to an end was one evening when we both were moderately intoxicated on wine, and she told me a story about her brother who was living with her prior to us getting married. Her brother was a casual drug user. She said one day her brother tried to get over on a big-time dealer without paying for his heroin. She said the dealer made threats to her and her brother about the consequences of not paying what her brother owed. She said out of the blue this dealer showed up unannounced at her home, and kicked the door down. He grabbed her and pinned her to the floor with a weapon at her throat, threatening to rape and kill her in front of her brother, demanding payment for the drugs her brother consumed. The dealer took her mortgage and utility money and left everyone unharmed. Emotionally, she was a wreck. Since that incident, she vowed to never be involved with nor to associate herself with anyone handling, dealing, or using drugs.

Immediately, my moderate intoxication was gone and I was overcome with fear. For months her story tormented me. I could not get the expression of terror in her eyes out of my head as she told me this story. The worst part for me was that she was trying to make a life with me, not knowing that the very person she vowed to stay away from was now her husband. We stopped talking to one another and experiencing life as a married couple only because I could not tell her the truth about my life, and therefore, I was causing our marriage to fail. I was not man enough to look into her eyes and tell her the truth about me and everything that I had been involved in since we met, especially after that night she told me about the incident with her brother.

One evening after a heated argument, we decided our marriage was over after being together almost eight months. The next day after our argument, I called her at work to tell her good-bye as I sat there on the living room floor of our ranch house. She did not have much to say and began weeping after several minutes of silence. I told her it was time for me to go, as I finished packing my things. I said good-bye to her once more as she continued to cry; and I hung up the phone, grabbed my things, and left. A week later, she called because she needed some money to pay some utility bills. That night I saw her for the last time. We talked for a little bit and tried to unravel all the issues in our marriage. Deep down, we both knew it was not going to work. She curled up on the bed, crying uncontrollably, as I grabbed my coat to leave. I placed a roll of 20-dollar bills on the end table. Since that night, I never looked back.

In spite of the marriage and separation, I continued to hustle and handle weapons. I was addicted to the act of being a dealer. The plan to slow down and get a grip never happened. Who was I fooling to ever think I would slow down? During the time that we were separated, I was still being tormented by her story and all the things I had done prior to the marriage and during the marriage. Years after we separated, even up to this day, neither she nor my family still do not know everything that I have done in my past.

At some point after the separation, I became ill in my body with hives. I could not sleep, even though I was extremely exhausted most of the time. I could not eat. I had no appetite. You would have thought I was on drugs from the amount of weight I had lost. I tried psyching myself out that I was not ill and that I was in control, but the more I tried to fool myself, the worse I'd become—

and then the fear began to take hold of me. I felt I was cursed from all of the drugs and weapons I sold that only advanced death upon hundreds, maybe even thousands of people. I kept saying and thinking to myself, *It is my turn to suffer for all the families and lives I helped destroy with my poison.* I thought I was going to die.

I tried to flee from this curse, illness, and fear through clubs, sex, or alcohol. I felt like I had no one to turn to and nowhere to go for help. I did not want my family to find out what I had been doing. I did not want them to see me in this lowly place I had found myself in, so I continued to hide from them. I would not go to a psychiatrist or a clinic because of my reputation and manly pride. I was not ready for church because I was committed to being a drug dealer. I was not ready to give up hustling for Jesus. I could not turn to the people that were selling for me because I did not trust them, even though I practically grew up with most of them. Not only that, if word got out about my condition, I would be finished in the streets as a drug dealer.

The clubs, sex, alcohol, and money were not enough to fix my issues. I needed something more, something stronger to escape this curse that plagued me with illness and fear. Then it happened. I became a victim of the very thing I feared most, my own products. I started getting high on my own drugs and not casually either. I would disappear for weekends at a time, calling off work—which was something I rarely did—just so I could get away and get high enough to somehow quiet or dull the demons that were speaking to me and placing this fear into my life. It seemed like the higher I got, the more I felt like I was becoming psychotic. I saw firsthand the power drugs had on people and how they could destroy relationships and families, and strip the esteem, pride, and dignity from a man or hardworking parents. I was in over my head now that I was using drugs. The fear I experienced of being killed or going to jail did not compare to the fear I experienced once I began to use drugs for myself. Not only did I fear becoming an addict, but also I had a constant battle in my mind each time that I got high of being a crackhead or letting my parents down again.

After several of months of abusing drugs and trying to escape my own thoughts, I somehow mustered the strength to stop myself from using drugs. Looking back, I know it was God. Even though I turned my back on Him, He didn't turn His back on me. And the truth of the matter is that there was no way I could control the addiction, let alone the fears in my life. For whatever reason, He was pulling me out of this phase of my life.

During the phase when I abused drugs, I felt myself giving into the high and giving up on myself each hour of each day I got high. For months I was craving, desiring, or even phening for that high, that feeling, that release. When I was high, it was like everything was going in slow motion with the mute button on. A glass could drop from the table, but it would seem like it took five minutes to fall and crash to the floor. I saw people but no faces. I heard conversations but no words. It was like I stood suspended in time between reality and nothingness. I was letting go of my life for this high. It was like I had sold my soul to the devil.

That is why I knew it had to be God who miraculously snapped me out of this state of floating between reality and nothingness. I had no idea how it happened or even why, but suddenly, I no longer had an appetite for that high. The very smell of crack cocaine burning or a lit joint made me ill to my stomach.

Just as soon as I got that taste for being high out of my mouth and put the drug abuse behind me, it was like getting high never even happened. I even denied or convinced myself that God had anything to do with delivering me from my condition. Why would He deliver me from my illness and drug abuse when it was me who turned my back on Him? I never stopped selling drugs and firearms, realizing that my ultimate addiction was my criminal lifestyle that I could not get away from. I would always make excuses as to why I was doing what I was doing. I was caught up in my criminal lifestyle and felt obligated to it.

6

Giving Up

I started not to care anymore about selling drugs, church, or myself. I couldn't rise above the demons and darkness in my life. In fact, I became so careless that members of my crew were stealing drugs and money from me, while others were becoming hard-core addicts. Though I didn't say it, deep down I wanted out of the game and didn't know how to simply quit. I was tired of hustling, lying, and hurting people. I was tired of the secrecy. I started praying that I would stop hurting people that could not control what they thought was under their control, even though I felt I had no control over stopping myself. Amazingly, I could stop doing drugs, but I could not stop selling them.

One late evening in the summer, I was out driving aimlessly by myself outside of the city limits of Cleveland with my cell phone and pager turned off and laying on the white leather passenger seat of my caddy. I heard a voice within myself say, "If you do not change your lifestyle, you will die before you turn 30 years old." I was 22 at the time. At first it startled me because this was not a thought that I was thinking to myself, and I was not high. This was an audible voice as if someone was sitting right next to me. I looked down at my cell phone to check and see if I left it on by chance, but my phone was indeed turned off. In a weird way, I thought God was strangely answering my prayer, but why would He talk to me like that? I convinced myself it was just me, and besides, I had time. A lot could happen in the next eight years. I kept hearing this over and over again in a very calm and gentle voice.

Deep down, I knew that a change was coming, but on the other hand, I could not avoid the part about death. I could not get that thought of dying before the age of 30 out of my mind. I had been shot at on a couple of different occasions, involved in gang related fights, chased by local police, and even by drug lords that I had robbed. I was able to accept the odds of possible death due to the crimes I was committing; but nothing was more frightening to me than to know that I could die an uncertain death at any moment, regardless if I committed a crime or not. I kept replaying over and over in my mind that at any time before I even reached 30 years of age I could die, not at 30, but before 30 years of age. I was terrified more than ever before.

Other hustlers and criminals would never tell you about their fears because it was the punk thing to do. There was no one I could turn to for advice or help, and my family was still unaware of my secret life, though they suspected something shady was going on. I didn't trust anyone that I grew up with or that was a part of my crew with what I was thinking and feeling, so I looked up this older guy I knew who helped me get started in the drug dealing business on a grand scale shortly after I graduated from high school. From time to time, I would stop at his place in this upper class community where very few people were allowed to visit, to talk to this older guy who had been in the game of hustling for many years before and after he was in prison. This older guy, in my eyes, was very wise and very intellectual. He accepted my request to meet him at his home.

I could never figure him out because he would always have women around him and at his home. These women that hung out at his home didn't look like the common prostitutes in the hood. These ladies looked like models; they didn't wear skimpy clothing or act ghetto. At first I thought he was a pimp, but it didn't quite make sense to me, and I didn't bother to ask. What I did ask him was about life in prison and how he kept his edge in the streets for as long as he did. He told me about his experience in prison, fears in the streets, and things I only wish I could have only asked him before I got ill and addicted to drugs. If you judged him based on how he carried himself, you would have never known that he dealt with being fearful. His exterior conveyed only control and confidence; he was mild tempered and soft spoken. He was a businessman who outside of the streets owned a car wash, a dry cleaning business, and several real estate properties.

As we talked, I was like a sponge, taking in everything he said. He was the only one who ever sat me down and was very transparent about being a hustler. He sat in his old English leather chair with the Isley Brothers softly playing in the background. He said that everyone that he knew in the street dealt with some type of fear. He said there comes a time when that fear is telling you something or flashing a caution sign, but we are too busy avoiding it or running from it to understand what the fear is actually saying. He said, therefore, we run and hide from fear instead of learning from it.

He took a sip from his glass, that he caressed in his right hand, and went on to say that hustling is not a career, but how I thought and what I thought were attributes were those of being a businessman, not a hustler. He said fear was telling me to get out of the game while I could and become a businessman, because once the game was over, it would be over for you. He said, "Never forget that while you are playing the game that there are others out there playing the same game, too. Some are younger, some are smarter; and many will do whatever it take to defeat you. Therefore, trust no one. Be very cautious and discreet wherever you go and with whatever you do." I quickly took his advice. I sat with him most of the night, listening, and strategizing in my head the next moves.

After I left his house, I decided to not drive along main traffic streets and highways during the day. I switched up cars to drive so that I would not be noticed. I only drove factory built cars with tinted windows, nothing customized or flashy. I would dress down my appearance with jeans and t-shirts. No gold chains, watches, and rings. I stopped dating for a while and bar hopping. I even scaled back on my points of drug distribution just to keep things manageable, while making the same amount of money, if not more, without as many people distributing for me. I gave up anything that would make me obvious to my enemies and the local authorities.

I am glad I had the chance to speak with him at the time that I did. Months later, he died in a drug sting operation at one of his homes, which turned into a violent shootout. However, I couldn't get away from the feeling of giving up. Now that I was reinventing myself based on what he said, I felt confused and conflicted within; and after I found out about his death, I really became distraught.

Late one cool summer night, I was on my way home from making my rounds. As I was driving up a semi-busy Cleveland street, the car in front of me started slowing down on the road I was traveling on. I noticed several cars ahead of me started turning onto the side streets before approaching the intersection that was about a half a mile ahead. Just a few blocks near the traffic light, I saw several blue, red, and yellow flashing lights in front of the line of cars before me. I just thought there must have been an accident or stalled car several vehicles in front of me. Cars were stopped in both directions, and police cars were lined up on one side of the street. As the line of cars crawled closer to the intersection, there were police officers scattered about by the curb of the street talking back and forth over their walkie-talkies.

I decided that I was going to turn around to take the side street, which is nothing unusual, but I couldn't. Officers blocked the last couple of side streets before the intersection as far as I could see. As the traffic in front of me began to slowly move again, and as I moved closer to the flashing lights, I realized that I was driving through a police staged sobriety checkpoint. Now, they were not just looking for drunk drivers, but they were looking for people with warrants, suspended driver's licenses, illegal drugs, and so forth.

This also gave the police a huge opportunity to profile. Being a young guy driving a caddy, I just knew I was going to get pulled over. Though I had no drugs present in this particular car, as cars passed through the checkpoint, an officer stood in front of my car, signaling me to pull into a parking area where other cars were parked and searched. I put the caddy in park as an officer stood near the driver's side door with a flashlight in his hand, asking me to exit so he could begin searching though my car. Another officer asked for my driver's license and proceeded to run my plates.

Before long, they went through my car. As they were searching, it dawned on me that my modified chrome-plated .380 handgun was hidden under the leather seats of my automobile. Even though I had a permit and the clip was not in the gun, the officer searching inside my car found my gun; and immediately, I was taken into custody. In Ohio, if you have a felony record, you are not permitted to carry so much as a butter knife, let alone a handgun in a public place, on your person, or in a vehicle, even if the firearm is registered. At the time, I was not aware of this law at all.

They cuffed me and read me my rights as they continued to search through my car. Then they asked if there was anything else they needed to be aware of, as they dumped my items out of my trunk onto the ground. I didn't respond. They carried me away into a transport vehicle filled with others who had broken the law, and we headed downtown to county jail again. As I rode in the back of this police van, handcuffed, I thought, *Here's my chance to get out of the game.*

I had a quick trial using a public defender, and I really did not care if I spent the next five years in jail or on probation. I did not hire a fancy lawyer and spend thousands of dollars to plead my case as I did before on my first conviction. I did not argue once with the judge. In fact, I said very little and so did my public defender. I just wanted the judge to carry out whatever sentence he was planning to issue me, even if that meant prison. After a brief recess, the judge sentenced me to jail. However, being as this was my second felony, instead of doing any jail time, the judge sentenced me to more probation with no jail time and said, "When you return to this court, and you will, I want to be here to personally throw the book at you." He said, "Three strikes and you will be out."

I was frustrated and tired of living in fear and kept thinking about what the older guy said about how hustling is not a career. I knew I had to do something about my life, and I did not want to see that judge ever again in my life. After I was dismissed from court, I remember standing outside of the rotating doors at the Justice Center in downtown Cleveland saying out loud to myself, "I am still alive, I am in my right mind, I am healthy; so what is stopping me from being an honest working man like my dad?

The following month after my court appearance, I visited the same parole officer, who still never asked if I had a job, or what was I going to do to be a good citizen. So one day out of nowhere, just before I completed my second probation term, I told him, "This will be one of the last times you see or hear from me again," knowing that my probation time was reduced. He stopped what he was doing with his paperwork and turned his chair to look straight into my eyes (which was the very first time he ever did that since my original conviction that I could recall). With this hard stare into my eyes and facial expression, he said what his mouth didn't, which was, "Oh yes, you will be back because this is about all you are worth." Then he sighed and went right back to his paperwork.

By the fall of 1993, I was fed up with myself and the life I was living. I was then a two-time convicted felon, college dropout, and separated from a woman who still had no idea of who I really was—all while I continued to lie to my parents, family, and friends. I began to desire freedom from being a drug dealer and living in secrecy and deception. I no longer cared about money, girls, cars, or hustling. I wanted to do something with my life and break this curse of fear I'd been living with. I wanted to stop this spiral downturn of events. I wanted to be proud of my life, not ashamed. During this time, and for the first time, I felt this was my only opportunity to overcome my urge to sell drugs and weapons and abandon my criminal lifestyle of destruction. I thought, *Here's my chance to be free from dying from within.* I was more determined than ever to put a stop to the lies once and for all.

7

Valley of Decision

Weeks had gone by since I had restocked any drugs, checked existing inventory, bagged, or distributed drugs. I had not even been in what I called the Kitchen, which was a crack house or place where I made crack cocaine, my most profitable product. I was moving one step closer to quitting; and I was kind of hopeful, nervous, and emotionally confused. However, I was second guessing myself about getting out of the game. My distributors were noticing changes also and were asking why I had not supplied them with more drugs to sell. I did not have an answer for them, or at least the answer I wanted to give them, because I was not ready to tell them that I was going to get off at the next stop. I wanted so badly to say, "I am done with being a drug dealer" and to walk away from it all, but the money kept calling me, as my mind was playing tricks on me. I felt anxiety and happiness at the same time.

Then one Sunday morning at one of my favorite eateries in Independence, Ohio, where I had brunch, I invited my closest members to dine with me at this high-end restaurant. It was that Sunday morning I sat at the head of the table with classical music playing softly in the background in the secluded banquet room. After we ate, the server came in to clear the table and then exited the room. I asked for everyone's attention. I took a moment to collect myself, and with a slight quiver in my voice, I announced that it was time for me get out of the game. Several people present were in disbelief over what they were hearing from my lips, and that went for me, too. They were trying to find every single reason for me to stay in the game, but the more they tried to convince me to stay in the business, the more determined I became to walk away from it all. I was trying to convince them that they should get out, too, before it was too late for them. Those who were determined to keep selling immediately went after my clientele; and before you knew it, it seemed as if everyone knew I was done selling drugs and firearms.

Months passed, the drug money was running low, and I was getting nervous. I was not used to being broke. I had to find a "real job" and fast since I quit the warehouse job where I distributed drugs for years. I did not want to be associated with that company or, better yet, I did not want to be tempted and then to relapse back into selling drugs. For once, I wanted to be a good citizen. I felt it in my bones, but I did not know what was required or how to go about it. I was in unfamiliar territory trying to be an honest man, so I did what I thought everyone else would do or should have done, especially in my situation.

I asked God to forgive me of my past and to guide me through the present changes in my life. I prayed to God and meant it. I decided to go back to church, which to this day was one of the greatest decisions I ever made. I remember when I was younger, it was at church that I was free; my life had meaning and purpose. When I was younger, even though everything I attempted did not go my way, I knew there was someone greater looking out for me. Deep down, I even thought that someone greater than myself was looking out for me even when I was in the streets.

Once again, I desired to be a part of my younger brother's life, who during all those years when I didn't go to church, he continued to go to church, even while he was in college. Unfortunately, my older brother's life had not changed much. He had been in and out of jail for the past several years, and I did not even know it. Both my parents were working more and more toward retirement.

At this point in my life, I knew what I had to do. That following Sunday, I walked up the stony steps of that Pentecostal inner-city church I used to faithfully attend and gave my life back to Christ, vowing to live with purpose. I forgave myself. I knew if I did not forgive myself, I would not have closure in my life. Finally, I learned to forgive my enemies, every drug dealer and every person that wanted to do me harm in the streets, especially the junkie that set me up that night. From that moment forward, I began living the reality of my dreams, to live like a good citizen. I became a registered voter. I had an official driver's license and other identification. I did not have to hide or be secretive about my life another day or minute. I no longer felt like I was less than human.

God was restoring the time I wasted in the streets and helping me to be a son to my parents and a brother to my brothers that I had neglected. I desired as never before to work a real job, to earn a paycheck, and to have a 401(k) with direct deposit.

Now that I was this new creature, I wondered, *What do I do now? I have no resume or any legal skill of interest that I could put on a resume. I dropped out of college, and I have a criminal record. Who is going to want this former drug-dealing entrepreneur?* I mean, I knew I was good at management because I had several people working under me dealing every day in the streets. I knew about asset management and managing profit and loss reports because that is what I studied during my limited time in college, and I had applied that knowledge to the criminal empire I once created. *How do I tell the employers of the bank the reasons why they*

should hire me, or why General Motors should give me a
chance, knowing all the mistakes I have made?

Application after application, rejection after rejection is how I found my way to this temporary agency office on the west side of Cleveland. The receptionist walked up and stood in the doorway of the cubical where I was taking my test. She knocked on the metal filing cabinet beside the doorway to let me know that I had about a minute left to complete and turn in my test. I sat there with the multiple choice test in front me, as I was in somewhat of a daze. After thinking over the past several years of my life, I got up from the brown metal folding chair with a grin on my face as I turned in the math test that I already completed. The receptionist asked what hours I could work and if I had reliable transportation. I told her what she wanted to hear, which was "I can work any shift and I'm available immediately." She said, "Okay,

Sugar, someone in our office will be contacting you this evening about a job; and good luck, Hun." For once, I was as excited as if had won something. I was proud of myself because I pushed beyond what I could not do for years. I left the temporary agency office, hopped into my caddy with a sigh of relief, and headed home to see my parents.

8

New Identity

When I was younger, I never once recall saying that I wanted to be a doctor, a lawyer, or a fireman when I grew up. However, I did believe I would be someone of importance, a leader of some sort in whatever area I chose. Somehow, through the good and the bad of my life, I always overcame challenges or circumstances, but why? What made me so special? Why did people trust me in the streets for direction? Whatever it was that others saw in me, I had to discover it for myself, which was a major key for me. I was always in the role of a leader, even though I was not purposely trying to be in the forefront, being the introvert that I was. Other people around me recognized my gifts, and for that reason, I would lead. Now that I knew that I had this gift of leadership, I had to get to know myself and to begin to develop this gift that I had been operating in, but now with structure. I took a couple of different personality profile tests which gave me great insight as to how I thought, how I behaved around people, and how I communicated. The more I understood the results of the different personality profile tests, the more I began to see myself in a totally new way, which also began to help me separate from my past identity.

Another thing that began to change was my perception. For instance, I no longer viewed a job as just a job. Rather, I saw every job or assignment I worked as a career path or a stepping stone to a greater future. As I began to dig deeper into the type of career path that I wanted to take, I remembered that when I was younger, other kids my age and even those that were older than me took well to my direction, whether that was finding a bike trail to ride on or selecting a neighborhood game to play. As a hustler, people leaned on me for instruction on how to operate a business, to make sure they had product, pricing, and clients. Then it became clear. All of the things I did in my childhood and how I conducted myself in the streets were aimed in the direction of being a manager, so management became the career I focused on.

On my new assignment through the temporary agency as a collector, I started observing employees and management. What were people's attitudes like toward the company and their colleagues? In every group, there was always someone who thought they knew it all but never get promoted. I learned a lot of what not to do from this type, like gossiping and brown-nosing. I even thought back to when I was working odd jobs and hustling how I learned a lot about the employee/manager relationship.

Employees respected managers that were promoted from within the company. The guy with a degree, hired from outside the company, who never worked a day at that company but was the boss over everyone who worked for the company 5, 10, 15, or more years often received a hard time from the employees he or she managed. The employees felt their new boss would never understand or appreciate what they had to do on a day-to-day basis. After thinking this over, I felt starting my career as an entry level collector was not so bad after all. If I worked hard and learned everything about the position, I was sure that I would get promoted to supervisor then manger and, eventually, director.

Well, what do you know? It worked. A few months after taking the temporary assignment and learning everything about the position, I was offered a permanent position as a collector. It only took a few months to achieve this status by learning from others' mistakes, as well as my own, while perfecting my knowledge of collections. I received award after award, bonuses, and other perks for being the rookie of this collection office. The temporary agency was even excited for me because I made them look good. They were proud to announce that they had several other candidates just like me, who were hardworking and eager to learn, lined up.

The company I was working for is one of the largest oil companies in the world. They were so pleased with my work that they wanted me to become a permanent employee. I was required to complete one of their applications, which I thought nothing of because they loved me there. Everything was great until I read on the application the question that has haunted me ever since I decided to become a good citizen: "Have you ever been convicted of a felony?" I convinced myself that this was not referring to me because, after all, they saw my hard work and discipline. I gained more awards than most of their permanent employees. I was always on time, if not early. I sacrificed hanging out, concerts, and dating to study for this permanent position. I even stayed late and on occasion took on additional tasks.

Not only did I NOT get the permanent position, but also, they cancelled my assignment as a temporary employee for them. For the first time in a very long time, I felt absolutely humiliated, angry, frustrated and disappointed. I could not believe they would not at least allow me to continue to work for them as a temporary employee. This was very difficult for me because I did not know who to turn to. My parents probably thought I was or should have been further along in my career than I really was since I stopped selling drugs. My older brother was in jail, and my younger brother was in college. I had no friends and no coworkers since they cancelled my assignment; and besides, I am sure my former coworkers found out what really happened, and I was probably just a joke to them. I thought about all the good I was doing and how much I had changed to become a better person, but I could not keep a job. When I got saved, Jesus took away the sin. I thought He was supposed to take away the felony charges, too. Not only that, I was broke and was beginning not to like the whole idea of being a good citizen. Even though the thought crossed my mind, there was no way I could live with myself as a hustler showing up to church, so going back to drug dealing was out.

9

Try and Try Again

I decided to give corporate America another chance, as if corporate America really cared. I took a new temporary assignment as a consumer debt collector for a different company, a Fortune 500 company. I was a little excited about this opportunity. After I did some research on this particular company, I discovered this company had been in business for over 150 years and had a good financial background and good leadership. Honestly, what had me at "hello" was this company employed more than 50,000 employees worldwide. See, I figured if and when they would hire me among that number of employees, there was no way I would be the only one with a felony record working for this corporate giant.

Like the previous job, I was an entry level collector, but this time with a little more experience. I studied everything I could about the Fair Debt Collection Practices Act and state collection laws, which varied if you were collecting in Minnesota or New Jersey. I learned everything I could to make myself and this company successful. Three months had passed, I was still an employee of the temporary agency that placed me with this company, and I started to lose hope that this company would offer me a permanent position. They were hiring people 45-60 days after placement. I thought I was a good employee. I came to work every day on time. Each month, I usually ranked among my colleagues as one of the top collectors.

Then I thought somehow they knew about my past or found out about my previous assignment and how they terminated my position and revoked their offer to hire me.

I had to snap myself out of that negative vibe and stinking thinking. There was more to my life than what I was currently experiencing, so every time things would not go as well as expected, I made it my mission to speak life to the situation—and more importantly, to speak life to my attitude.

Several days later, I was called into the director's office. I sometimes wondered if my director was bipolar. One minute, she was happy, joking, and laughing with the staff, serving up high fives; and then, bam, just like that, she was militant and super serious, with eyes that stared through you like red hot lasers. When she called me into her office, she requested that I be seated. With a stern face and monotone voice, she made some small talk and then afterwards, I was free to return to my desk to resume working.

The very next day, I was offered a position as a permanent employee for this Fortune 500 company. I was beyond excited and at a loss for words about my permanent position making only eight dollars an hour, but I knew this was only the beginning of something good. I was also excited because a lot of the people I witnessed going into the director's office were not getting promoted. That day I kind of knew what it would have felt like to hit the lottery; and for a second, I even forgot that I once had a criminal record.

The next day, the assistant director sat me down to congratulate me and then slid a four-page application across his oak desk. In order to become a part of this organization, I had to complete this application that required a state and federal background check, credit reports to be pulled, and I had to take a mandatory drug test. I picked up the application with my nervous fingers; I excused myself from his office to get a pen from my desk and to cry out, "Oh God, why have you forsaken me???" Because I knew the question that I dreaded to answer would be on the application. The drug test was the easy part because I had not touched or even looked at drugs for some time. It was the background check that I was worried about. Once I settled down somewhat and filled out the application with my twitching, nervous fingers, I made up my mind that, *If this does not work out, I am definitely going back to hustling.* I knew that it was not what I wanted to do, but in the hood I did not have to submit an application or have background checks done to be a drug dealer. However, deep down, I really believed that I was a changed person and fought even harder to speak life.

It took about four days to get the results back; and for about four days, I had never been so close to God.

About four days later, I was pulled into the director's office. With a stern face and monotone voice, my director congratulated me and presented me with a company handbook and other paperwork for my new permanent position. I had a job with benefits, a 401(k), vacation time, and yes, direct deposit. I felt like I had truly won the battle over the thought of honest living versus drug dealing, good over evil. Even though corporate America compared to hustling was definitely more stressful and the reward was not as great, I felt a level of importance in my life, a sense of belonging.

10

Climbing the Ladder

It wasn't long after being hired from the temporary position to a permanent one that I became a team leader. I went from Team Leader to Team Captain. That following year, I was named Collection Supervisor for the Cleveland office. I was on the fast track to success. I was extremely excited because people noticed my performance and not my past. I am a living witness that people can change. Since I was in management, it was somewhat awkward being trained by the supervisor that I was then equal to. Now, the best part about this was this all happened with two felony records and no college degree. People who I sat with every day at work were stunned, though some would say they saw it in me all along. Oddly enough, not one person ever asked me,

"How did you do it? How did you start from a temporary assignment as an entry level worker and become a collection supervisor for an office of 60 or more collectors?" If they would have asked me, "How did you do it?" this is what I would have told them:

1. Discover yourself. Get to know who you are, what you like to do, and what you can do effortlessly. Things that come easy to you would most likely be the things you will enjoy and enjoy getting paid to do.

2. Discover and develop the gifts you possess. If you are or want to be a manager, read books about management, take courses in leadership, and attend business seminars. Even if you are in an entry level position, you have to turn your focus on being a manger, not some minimum wage worker. Get to know and

hang around people who are managers, business owners, and professionals. This is the best mentoring you will ever receive—listen and learn what to do and what not to do from others' successes and mistakes. Study how professionals behave, what they wear, what they often talk about, read, and participate in. A good place for this is business networking meetings and luncheons held by the Chamber of Commerce.

3.   Have a plan. Write it down and remind yourself this is what you will accomplish this month, year, or while you're employed with this company.

4.   Know the career you have chosen. If you are a sales or customer service representative, know your products; learn how to listen and be

patient. If you're in sales, build rapport with your customers, learn the buying signals, how to make the offer, and how to close the deal. If you are a customer service rep, do not take irate situations personally. Listen to the customer, and offer options to solve their problem.

5. Once you have discovered yourself, your gifts, and know what type of career you want to pursue, surround yourself with people who will speak life into your vision. Do not allow anyone to tell you that you cannot do whatever comes naturally or effortlessly to you or let anyone tell you that you will not be successful. The past should only remind you of how much better your future is going to be each and every moment that passes, starting right now.

6. A good helper is a good leader. Be willing to work late sometimes, or to fill in for someone who called off. Be willing to take on additional work, even if you do not get recognized or paid for it. Your efforts will not go unnoticed.

7. Finally, be proactive. Take the initiative to try something new or to carry out a thought to make something better, even if it fails. Do this because a good manager does not only look at your success, but also they look at who is willing and reliable and who is a risk taker.

Prior to getting promoted, I watched the director operate and manage this collection office very closely. I wanted to know his daily work agenda from the time he was in the office until he left for the day. I wanted to know what his goals were; and once I discovered what they were, I began to make his goals for the company my goals, too. The director was always looking for ways to be more efficient, to streamline his operations, and to be profitable at the same time. I did this not to be a brown-noser, but I knew if I hung around him long enough to be mentored by him, I would one day be his successor as Director of Operations for the Cleveland Collection Division of this company.

I was often told in the past that turkeys do not fly with eagles. If you are an eagle, then surround yourself with other eagles. An eagle for me is someone who is like-minded and actively productive, or is in a leadership role that is in-line with the career I desire to achieve. Like a sponge, I learned from him how to find needs in a company and to come up with ideas to create solutions.

No executive wants to hear about problems the company is facing. They want to hear about solutions to those problems, especially how you, the employee and staff, are going to take an active role to fix it and not leave it up to the executive to solve. If a company is losing money, they do not want to hear about money being lost, but they want to know how the management staff could be more efficient, save money, and reduce waste. They want an optional approach to drive in sales and boost customer service; and they are expecting management to come up with those answers and to be prepared to act. They do not want suggestions.

That became my mission, to find ways to improve the efficiency of the company and to be a problem solver. Although I felt like I was out of their league in so many ways, I had to equip myself with the knowledge to handle this mission, so I started taking seminars and classes on my own time. I read a variety of books on how to be a manager, how to be a people person, delegating, creating an atmosphere of excitement in the office, and developing strong working relationships. Over time, I gained the confidence and knowledge within myself, along with the experience, to be just as effective as a degreed college graduate.

11

Making a Way

The past few months had been huge months for the collection office in Cleveland. Every goal and forecast set for the past months was defeated by great percentages. One day the director was doing his usual work, reviewing reports, charts, and graphs to understand what he must do to be more effective, efficient, and profitable. Our collection office was always ranked in the top three in the country next to Atlanta and Chicago for the highest dollars collected each month. Why was it so important that the director would come to work every day a couple of hours early and brainstorm on what he could do to be number one in the nation?

For me, this was my time to shine. I once heard that the fastest way to get promoted in a company is to understand the needs of a company, and then find a solution for those needs. I took in everything the director said and everything he was brainstorming on, gathered the opinions of the other supervisors and managers, and suddenly, the light came on. As a collection office we were strong at performance, but we lacked the ability to see strengths and weaknesses on a daily basis for each collector who made this office powerful in collections each month. Therefore, management was not able to provide the support and training based on each collector's ability to perform.

So I began to create spreadsheets to track performance and areas needing improvement. I created a list of responses to monitor if the collector properly introduced himself, stated why they were calling, provided any legal detail, etc. I monitored the collectors' tones and the pitch of their voices for professionalism, how they overcame rebuttals, and when to request payment, along with the average time it took to collect from the debtor. I then created a point system that would reward collectors for being compliant with the list of responses, collection guidelines, and company policies. Finally, I established quality control measures for the Cleveland office to show how to collect the same amount of money in less time, which ultimately allowed the office to call on more debtors, which would increase our month-end collections. I was walking on eggshells because I never once asked for permission to take on this project. Most of the time I spent on this project was on my own personal time. Neither management nor my director had a clue as to what I was doing.

Early one morning prior to my shift, I met the director at his office and presented this project I had been working on for the past few weeks to him. I knocked on his office door that was already opened. He invited me in from the doorway. I brought in my folder with several spreadsheets full of data and reports I had compiled. I spread out the sheets on his desk. As he put on his reading glasses, with his coffee cup nearby, he leaned forward to view the sheets I laid out in front of him. There was a total dead silence in the office as I stood there watching him review my project. He sat there for about five to ten very long minutes staring at the paperwork I gave him, with his index finger resting on his nose and his hand covering his chin. From his silence and pensive look, I could not tell whether he was angry, confused, or if I had simply just wasted his and my time.

Minutes after the awkward silence in his office, while I watched him sit in the same position reading my project, the director sat back into his high-back leather chair and began to look at me for a few seconds the same way he was looking at my project, but it felt like two minutes. The director leaned his body toward me over his desk and said very calmly that he absolutely loved my idea. He said he could not help but to feel a bit embarrassed because he never actually thought about doing what I presented. He said this project could streamline the way business had been conducted and potentially make the company more profitable.

Initially, the director said he wanted me to run this project by the management staff first. Then he stopped himself in the middle of his sentence and said, "I guess we are going to have to create a title for this upper management position." In other words, he wanted me to head this project up, me! He wanted me to run this department. I became light-headed, with butterflies in my stomach, but quickly got control of myself. But I wanted so badly to break-dance or get my praise on in the middle of his office.

Who's the man?! I finally made it to upper management. I am on top of my game. I am stomping with the big dogs. However, there was one thing I did not realize until the announcement of my new title and position was made. I had to have another background check, credit check, and drug test all over again because I was no longer considered an hourly employee but a salaried executive. "No big deal," I said to myself. "They will not find anything negative on me now; my background is the same as when they first hired me. I have not touched any part of drugs, not even a poppy seed muffin, since I had been consistently attending church, which has been about four years at this point." I filled out the executive packet for my new position the same way I did when I became a permanent employee.

I had to wait four days for my results, as before. In the meantime, I was operating under this new executive position as Quality Assurance Director. It was happening for me. I had my window office and was making good money. The day had finally come for me. The results of my background check, credit check, and drug test were back. The director discovered my past history from the results of the test. He took me outside and sat me down at a picnic table near the office building parking lot and said, "Everyone has a past, whether it's on paper or not." He said, "There are tons of people breaking the law and committing felonies every day but who have not been caught yet."

You know, that turned on the light for me. He was right. Everyone has done something that they are not proud of, thinking back to my days as a dealer and all the honest looking people who were doing drugs or other malicious acts and had never been caught. Everyone does have a past or a testimony of how they overcame life. I was honored because there was no way I could have been in that position despite my past and still have a job. I was ecstatic and very grateful.

It had been about nine months since my promotion. In spite of the collection office's continual improvements and increase in collections each month, the company as a whole was not doing very well. Across the country, the company decided to cut back its staff. They announced they were downsizing up to 30 percent of its office personnel due to financial reasons as a whole. This company employed 50,000 employees worldwide; 30 percent to be downsized was a little over 10,000 employees in the U.S. alone. One of the major cuts that shocked me, and even surprised the employees of the collection office, was that they downsized the director. This stunned me because due to the direction and leading of the director, the Cleveland office made this branch even more successful than it already was. Not to mention, he helped me to rise above my past promotion after promotion.

Days later, after he was officially removed from his position and the company, there was a new person in power as the director. All employees had to be re-interviewed, regardless of how long they had worked for the company. And guess what? We had to complete another four-page application. The difference with the new person is that he was a robot with no emotion. The odds were against him because he needed to get himself out of the shadow of the previous director, and he did whatever it took to do so. This person's goal was to eliminate 20-25 percent of the office staff, which would ultimately make him look good for reducing a company's greatest expense, payroll, while demanding the same level of productivity with a reduced staff. By achieving that stage of the plan, it would increase profitability.

I soon learned the most expensive payroll of any company is management, which also meant that everything I worked for was about to be gone, and so it was. I was given the option to stay on board with the company; however, my pay would be reduced, and I would go back to hourly pay, even though I would be required to produce the same type and amount of work. I stayed on for a few months, while also picking up a part-time job at a call center working evenings. I had to do something to offset my decrease in pay.

The operations manager at the call center said there was something different about me and felt I was overqualified to work a part-time position and requested my resume. Weeks later, I was offered a call center management position, making me the number three person in charge of the call center that employed over 160 people. *I made it*, I thought to myself, *because I presented myself well; and for once, I did not start from the bottom.* I had favor and doors were opening for me, and it was exciting. Regardless of my ups and downs, I knew no matter what would happen, I was protected.

A couple of months later, the operations manager resigned to work for a credit card company; and there was no one more qualified than me at the time to take on this position, which came with more responsibilities but a greater salary. I soon was named Operations Manager.

Months later, after taking the number two position, the director of operations decided she was going back to school and resigned to follow her dreams; and shortly after, I accepted the number one position and became the director for this call center. I had developed a very good relationship with the company vice-president, whom I clung to as my mentor. I also was mentored by the Human Resources director, who taught me how to write company policies and employee handbooks. Also, I learned alternative ways to conduct performance evaluations and enforce disciplinary actions.

But if I dig a little deeper into my past life, I realized that I have been mentored by someone all along. I learned wisdom from the older guy about surviving as a hustler. His experience in the streets taught me the knowledge I needed to be successful as a drug dealer. He took me under his wing and taught me how to protect myself, how to be a salesman, and how to identify people with whom you want to do business. In addition, the older guy taught me how to read profit and loss statements, and how to manage a business.

Overall, the knowledge I gained in the streets and in the office environment developed me to become the driven person that I am. Knowledge is knowledge, no matter where you gain it from. How you apply knowledge determines if you really learned anything.

12

The Journey in Life

From this point in my career, I continued to climb the ladder of corporate America. It had been nearly a year since I had been employed as Director of the call center. There were rumors throughout the center about the financial strength of this company and how the company was planning to close the center over the following 18 months. They were planning to shut down 20 percent of its operation in the next few months due to poor store sales performance for the past three quarters. I did not believe it to be true since the call center was doing very well and the rating for client satisfaction was good, if not better than the prior year's stats. Then I became a believer after I met with the Human Resources director who sat me down to discuss my options.

Options? Then it dawned on me that I, too, was being downsized.

I had mixed feelings regarding being downsized. On the one hand, I was sad because my department performed very well and I enjoyed my work and my employees. My department was efficient and overall saved the company money based on smart choices made under my direction at the call center. However, the call center did not generate income for the company. Its function was to support the stores that do. I truly understood their decision to downsize me, along with several others, at the call center. Interesting enough, prior to the announcement, I was given the offer to work on the store side of the company instead of the call center portion of it. Now I understood why. The company was shifting its focus and drive into building up the sales force within the stores in order to make themselves profitable as a whole again.

Now on the other hand, I was excited about being downsized because I felt it was an opportunity for me to take a much-needed vacation. I had been giving so much of myself to building a career that I failed to reward myself with time off, to get a life outside of work, and to be with my family. The company offered a very good severance package, so I was able to take a few months off. After traveling and spending time with my family and friends, I had to figure out my new career path. I mean, I could have worked for another call center or collections office, but I wanted to be more diversified in management.

It was a few days after the 9/11 terrorist attack that I ended up accepting a position for a Fortune 200 company where I started off as an assistant manager for this major retail chain. The attack on 9/11 not only affected the national security of our country, but also it was a sharp blow to businesses across the board, especially retail. Sales and walk-in traffic were down sharply compared to the past few years' sales records. Competitors were closing down part of their retail operations or simply going out of business due to the lack of consumer spending going into the holiday season, which was the most profitable season of the year.

In spite of the tragedy of 9/11, I worked very hard at my position and management noticed. My goal was to get accepted into the fast track program to become the next district manager out of the Cleveland market. I went from Assistant Manager of a $500,000 store that turned into a million dollar store, to getting a promotion to Store Manager of a multimillion dollar store, to getting accepted into the District Manager Training program. This all took place within 18 months of being employed by this company. I loved what I did but was not feeling the extensive travel and, even more, the mandatory hours I had to work, especially on the weekends.

After almost three years with the Fortune 200 Company, I gave my two weeks' notice in order to pursue a career with a regional retail company as a district manager. After one year of working for the regional retailer, I was named Vice-President of Sales and Marketing for the company, being the number two person in command. I thought *Wow, I never thought I would ever get this far working for a company that grosses millions of dollars each month.* I was on my way to achieving my greatest desire of owning my own business. Being Vice-President of this regional retail business was a dream come true, but it was not my final destination. It was just another point in my journey to bringing me full circle to where I am now, writing this book about my life in corporate America.

Do not let your past be the end of your journey in life. You can still make your dreams a reality as long as you are willing to put forth the work and the time it takes to realize your dreams. I am a living testimony that you do not have to be haunted by your past, but you can learn from your past and make better choices for a better future. "And we know [with great confidence] that God [who is deeply concerned about us] causes all things to work together [as a plan] for good for those who love God, to those who are called according to His plan and purpose" (Romans 8:28, Amplified Bible version).

It is not about the positions I was able to obtain but about the journey. Each phase of my journey built my faith in God and my confidence in myself that I could do great things. It was a journey of recovery and rediscovery. It was not an easy journey for me, but it was definitely fruitful for me. I am now remarried. Can you image? It's been over 20 years since my wife and friend has been married to me. I gave up the streets to live the good life. I have three young and beautiful children, a girl and two boys. My life has been utterly changed, and better yet, redeemed. No longer do I live in fear or walk along the path of destruction. And guess what? My journey is not over. I am excited to see what's in store for me in this new phase of my life.

What story will you write? Premature death or being locked in prison is no longer an option when you have nothing but opportunity staring you in the face. If a college dropout and two-time felon can make it as a vice president and now business owner, what is your excuse? Learn from my experience, and create your own success or destiny. Do not allow your past to define who you are as a person or what you can do now to create the future you desire for yourself and your family. You can change and change for good. It is up to you. I pray that you will allow my life to be an encouragement and to help as you begin your own journey from a dirt road to smooth pavement.

www.LiveDailey.com

www.ingramcontent.com/pod-product-compliance
Lightning Source LLC
Chambersburg PA
CBHW070320190526
45169CB00005B/1678